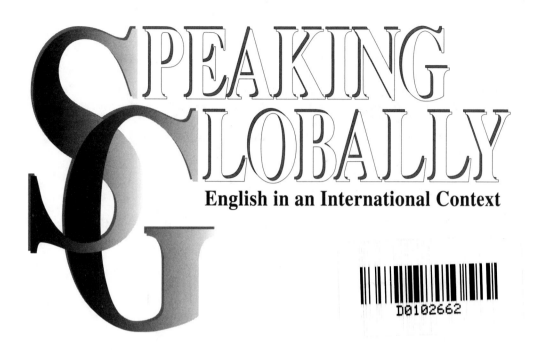

SPEAKING GLOBALLY

English in an International Context

WILLIAM GROHE • CHRISTINE ROOT

PRENTICE HALL REGENTS

Editorial Director: *Arley Gray*
Manager of Development Services: *Louisa Hellegers*
Director of Production and Manufacturing: *Aliza Greenblatt*
Manager of Production/Design: *Dominick Mosco*
Interior Design, Page Composition, and Electronic Art: *Ken Liao*
Cover Coordinator: *Merle Krumper*
Manufacturing Buyer: *Ray Keating*

Illustrations: *Hugh Harrison* and *Kathy Hebert*

Printed in the United States of America

10 9 8 7 6 5 4

ISBN 0-205-15600-2

Table of Contents

Introduction

Speaking Globally is a student-centered, collaborative discussion/conversation book for adults at the intermediate level who are learning English as a second or foreign language. It is meant for students, businesspeople, professionals, and travelers from all over the world. The content is designed to produce lively, meaningful discussion on matters of international interest and concern. The goals of the text are to help students develop their discussion and presentation skills, to foster intercultural understanding, to develop independent research skills in English, and to sharpen critical thinking skills.

The text is organized thematically around areas of international importance. An illustration at the beginning of each unit serves as an introduction to the topic and as a springboard to discussion. Background readings add context, vocabulary, and information to the discussions. The "Synthesis Project," the main focus of each unit, provides an opportunity for students to research a topic of personal interest as they work through the unit. Then, they present the topic orally to the class. Guidelines for giving an oral presentation and discussion strategies are provided. The "Speaking and Thinking Critically" section of each unit contains a case study in which students work together in small groups to solve a hypothetical problem. Each unit concludes with a "Journal Entry" to help students pull together their own thoughts and opinions on the subject of the unit.

It is our intention that the topics and guided exercises presented in *Speaking Globally* will foster discussions that are important and relevant to students, so that they feel a sense of accomplishment and intellectual growth as they progress in English fluency. We hope that *Speaking Globally* will open the door to greater understanding and appreciation among people of different backgrounds.

Dedication

To our children—Brian, Ian, Matthew, and Michelle—who we hope will live in a world of tolerance and understanding, and our spouses—David and Modjgan—who have shown tolerance and understanding during the time spent on this project.

SPEAKING GLOBALLY

English in an International Context

UNIT **1**

International English

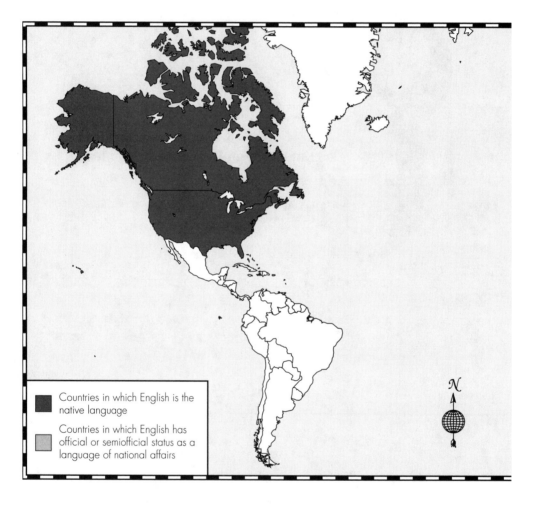

Countries in which English is the native language

Countries in which English has official or semiofficial status as a language of national affairs

1. In what countries is English the native language?
2. In what countries is English used as the official language?

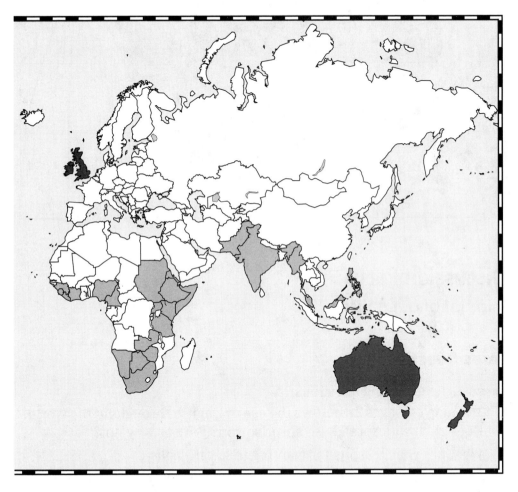

Presentation Strategy: Gathering information through interviews

Discussion Strategy: Introductions • Getting to know people

Discussion Focus
International English

Focus Questions

Discuss the following questions.
1. The map on pages 2–3 shows the use of English throughout the world. Does such widespread use surprise you? Why or why not?
2. What are your reasons for wanting to learn English?
3. In the future, do you think everyone will learn English? Why or why not?
4. Do you think that you need to learn the culture of a people along with their language to communicate with them? Why or why not?
5. If a Korean businessman is doing business in Germany with a German, and they are using English as their common language, is it

important for them to understand American or British culture to communicate? Why or why not?

Background Reading 📼

Read the following article. Then complete the exercise that follows.

English is the most widely spoken language in the world today. There are estimates, in fact, that nearly one billion (1,000,000,000) people speak English.[1] When we say "English," however, we are really talking about many different dialects of English. American English, British English, Indian English, and Philippine English are just a few examples of different English dialects. Each dialect has its own unique vocabulary, usage, and pronunciation patterns. Dialects are similar, and usually people from two different dialects can communicate with each other as long as they don't use idioms or slang words unique to their native dialects.

With the growing use of English in such areas as international business, international travel, science, and technology, the new term "English as an International Language" is emerging. Think about the following situation: If a Thai businessman is doing business with a Saudi Arabian in Italy, the chances are good that they would have their discussions in English. What dialect of English would they use? They probably wouldn't use any of the native dialects of English. However, people can and do communicate, using "International English." Millions of people all over the world speak English as an international language. International English is unique because it doesn't share common idioms, slang, pronunciation patterns, or usage with any one other English dialect.

dialect the language used by a particular community, region, or social group

usage the particular way a word or phrase is used

emerging beginning to develop

Class Discussion

Discuss the following questions with your classmates.

1. Do you think learning American idiomatic expressions is necessary in an English class in the United States? What about an English class in Malaysia? Why or why not?

2. According to the article on page 5, what makes a dialect unique? Are there any other factors that makes one dialect different from another?

3. The article says that a person learning to use English for international purposes can communicate without learning a native dialect of English. Do you think this is true? Why or why not? What is your experience with English dialects?

4. Do you think linguists should study "International English" and try to simplify it so that people can learn it more quickly and easily? Why or why not? How?

5. English is used as a second language in many countries. For example, millions of people in India learn English so they can communicate with other Indians who speak other languages. Can you think of other countries where English is used as a second language?

Presentation Strategy
Gathering Information through Interviews

Synthesis Project

Interviews are one way to gather information from several different people. To conduct an interview, you ask questions about a specific topic.

1. Interview at least two people who are not in your class but who have learned English as a second or an international language. Ask them their views on learning a new language in general and the English language in particular.

2. Before the interviews, write down on note cards the questions that you plan to ask. Leave some space between each question so that you

can quickly take notes. Don't try to write down every word that each person says. Instead, write down the main ideas and key words.

3. Be prepared to share the information that you gather in a three-minute presentation that you will give when you finish this unit.

Discussion Strategy

Introductions

Getting to Know People

Introductions are the first step in the process of getting to know people. In this book you and your classmates will be discussing many topics. Therefore, it is very important that you get to know each other before you talk about any of the issues presented.

1. Introduce yourself to your classmates. Tell them your name and something about you, such as what your native country is. Then talk about why you are studying English.

2. After you introduce yourself to your classmates, sit down with a partner and interview each other. Share more detailed information about yourselves. You may talk about your family, your hobbies, your work, or your other interests. Use the space below to write down some of the things your partner tells you.

_____

_____

_____

3. Take a few minutes to prepare a short statement about your partner. Write down the main ideas and important points. Don't worry about punctuation and spelling. What is important is that you are able to understand the main points of what your partner says. Then, introduce your partner to the rest of the class.

Speaking and Thinking Critically

Reacting to Information

Work with a partner. Read the statements below and discuss the questions that follow each statement.

> More people speak English as an international or second language than speak English as their native language. In China alone, more people are learning English as an international language than there are people who live in the United States.[2] About 330,000,000 people speak a dialect of English as their native language[3] (in the United Kingdom, the United States, Canada, Australia, New Zealand, South Africa,

and the West Indies), while about 400,000,000 people speak English as a second language[4] (in India, Kenya, the Philippines, and Nigeria).

1. What is your reaction to these facts?

2. What are some historical reasons that caused this situation to occur?

English has many dialects—for example, British English, American English, Canadian English, Indian English, Jamaican English, Australian English, and Philippine English.

3. Do you think International English should be one of these dialects or none of them? Why or why not?

English is the primary international language used in science, technology, business, air and sea travel, and diplomacy.

4. Which of these areas is the most important for you now?

5. Will other areas become more important for you as time passes?

English is used as an official language in forty-four countries, more than any other language.[5] In fact, approximately 80 percent of the information stored in computers is written in English.[6] Approximately 75 percent of the mail, cables, and telexes that are sent around the world are in English.[7] And, about 50 percent of all scientific and technical journals are written in English.[8]

6. Do these statistics surprise you? Why or why not?

Discussing Alternatives

You have already made a decision to improve your English by attending this class. In small groups, think of specific ways to improve your English and list them below.

Method One:

_____

_____

_____

Method Two:

_____

_____

_____

Method Three:

_____

_____

_____

Making a Decision

Decide with your group which method you came up with in the previous section is best. Share your group's suggestions and choice of the best method for improving your English with the rest of the class.

Putting It All Together

Giving an Oral Presentation

In a three-minute presentation, share the information you gathered from your interviews with people not in your class. Use the notes you took during the interviews to help you remember the main points you want to make concerning people's opinions about learning a new language in general or about learning English in particular. Try not to read the notes word for word to the class.

Writing a Journal Entry

After each student gives his or her presentation, write down your thoughts, opinions, reactions, and questions in the journal below. Your journal entries will help you organize your thoughts about the topics in this book.

Journal

In small groups, you might want to discuss some of the ideas that you have written in your journal.

International Travel

Presentation Strategy: Summarizing

Discussion Strategy: Discussing the Pros and Cons of an Issue

Discussion Focus
International Travel

Focus Questions

Discuss the following questions.

1. Where have you traveled? What were your favorite places? What were your least favorite? Why?
2. How has international travel changed the world?
3. Has international travel changed you? How?

Background Reading 📼

Read the following facts about travel today. Then complete the exercise that follows.

- Travel/Tourism is the world's largest industry.[1]
- About $2.4 trillion ($2,400,000,000,000) is spent worldwide on travel/tourism each year.[2]
- In a recent year, tourists made 400 million trips abroad.[3]
- The most popular tourist destination in the United States for both domestic and international travelers is Disney World in Orlando, Florida.[4]
- The city with the most hotel rooms in the United States is Orlando, Florida.[5]
- Over 470,000 Japanese tourists visited Canada in a recent year.[6]
- Japanese visitors to Canada spent an average of $180 a day; German visitors to Canada spent an average of $74 a day.[7]
- Recently, the Malaysian government spent $33 million in one year to attract international tourists; the Spanish government spent $32 million attracting international tourists the same year.[8]

> • An average of 250,000 international tourists visit Nepal every year.[9]

Class Discussion

Look at the following statements. Then follow the directions as indicated.

1. Use the facts above about travel and tourism to write two questions. You can write specific questions about the facts themselves or more general questions about your classmates' own experiences.
2. In small groups, ask your classmates the questions you have written. The student in the group who answers a question asks the next question. Look at the example.

> **Student A:** Did you know that travel/tourism is the world's largest industry?
>
> **Student B:** No, I didn't. That fact surprised me. How important is travel/tourism in your country?
>
> **Student C:** Very important. It is our number one industry.

Presentation Strategy
Summarizing

Synthesis Project

Summarizing is the process of taking the main ideas and important points about a topic or issue and presenting them clearly to an audience.

1. Interview someone not in your class who has travelled internationally. Find out as much information as you can about one of his or her trips.
2. Before the interview, write down on note cards the questions that you plan to ask. Here are some sample questions to get you started:
   - When did your trip begin and how long was it?
   - What was the purpose of the trip?

- Where did you stay?
- What interesting things did you see?
- What were the people like?
- How was the food?
- What did you like about the trip?
- What did you dislike about the trip?
- Ask your own questions.

Remember to leave some space between each question so you are able to take notes during the interview. You don't have to write down everything the speaker says, but be sure to get important details and not just the main ideas. If necessary, repeat your questions in order to get important details. Look at the example.

Student A: When did you leave Narita airport?

Student B: I arrived at the airport at about 6:00 in the morning, but the plane was delayed so I didn't actually leave until four hours later.

Student A: So you left at about 10:00?

Student B: That's correct. And I was angry about the delay.

1. When you summarize, present only the important points. For example, the preceding dialogue could be summarized as follows: *Student B* arrived at Narita airport at 6:00 A.M. The plane was delayed four hours. She actually left at 10:00 A.M.

2. Revise, organize, and summarize your notes so that you can be prepared to give a three-minute oral presentation when you finish this unit.

Discussion Strategy
Discussing the Pros and Cons of an Issue

When you consider the pros and cons of an issue, you are looking at the good or strong points (pros) and the bad or weak points (cons) of that issue. By considering both the pros and the cons of an issue, you are better able to understand and discuss the issue. For instance, if you consider the impact of increased international travel on different cultures around the world, you can point out the pros and the cons of the impact. Look at the example.

Pros

- International travel has brought people together from different cultures.
- International travel has helped the global economy.

Cons

- International travel has caused an increase in intercultural misunderstandings.
- Increased international travel has caused more global pollution.

1. In small groups, consider the impact of increased international travel on different cultures around the world. How has international travel affected your countries? Write down some of the pros and the cons.

Pros

- _____
- _____
- _____

Cons

- _____
- _____
- _____

2. In small groups discuss the impact of international travel on different cultures around the world. Note that what one person considers a "pro" someone else may consider a "con."

3. Have one member of your group summarize the group's discussion for the class. The speaker should point out the pros and the cons the group came up with, and any conclusions you reached.

Speaking and Thinking Critically

Reacting to Information

Work with a partner. Take turns asking and answering the following questions. Take notes as your partner speaks, and be sure to consider the pros and cons of each question. Then share your notes in small groups.

1. Many governments have spent millions of dollars attracting international tourists. Do you think this is a good or bad government policy? Why?

    _____

    _____

    _____

2. Many international tourists visit Nepal. Is this good or bad for Nepal? Why?

    _____

    _____

    _____

3. About $2.4 trillion is spent on travel/tourism each year. Speaking globally, how is this good and bad for the world in general? Why?

    _____

    _____

    _____

Summarize your notes for the rest of the class. Then discuss the questions with your classmates.

Discussing Alternatives

In small groups, read the following case study about a country's declining tourism industry and the solutions recommended to solve the problem. Then discuss the pros and cons of each solution. If you don't like any of the recommendations given, suggest other possibilities.

Case Study

The island nation of Fibaluba gets approximately 90 percent of its revenue from tourism. The only other industries in the country are the pineapple and coconut industries. During the past three years tourism has been steadily *declining*, which has seriously hurt the national economy. There has been much discussion among Fibaluba's leaders about why tourism has been in decline. Some people *blame* the decline on the 8 percent sales tax that tourists must pay on everything they buy. Others *claim* that there isn't enough for tourists to do; the island is beautiful, but there isn't much nightlife. Others feel that the residents are not friendly enough. Everybody agrees that something needs to be done as soon as possible to attract more tourists. The following solutions are under consideration:

Recommendation 1: Cut the sales tax in half, to 4 percent. This would reduce the amount of revenue per tourist, but it would (they hope) increase the number of tourists.

Recommendation 2: Open up government-owned *casinos*. This would give tourists something to do at night, and it would also increase government revenue.

Recommendation 3: Start a *campaign* to encourage the residents to be friendlier. Begin educational programs to teach them the importance of tourism and their role in attracting tourists. Also offer *cash awards* to local people who are especially friendly and helpful to tourists.

Recommendation 4: Think of your own solution.

revenue income

declining decreasing

blame to find fault

claim   declare

casino   a place used for gambling

campaign   an organized movement with a specific goal

cash award   money

Now discuss the pros and cons of each recommendation. Be sure to take notes during the discussion.

Recommendation 1

Pros

_____

_____

_____

Cons

_____

_____

_____

Recommendation 2

Pros

_____

_____

_____

Cons

_____

_____

_____

Recommendation 3

Pros

_____

_____

_____

Cons

_____

_____

_____

Recommendation 4

Pros

_____

_____

_____

Cons

_____

_____

_____

Making a Decision

Summarize the pros and cons of each of the recommendations you discussed in the previous section. Discuss the recommendations within your group, and then decide which is the best solution to Fibaluba's financial problems.

_____

_____

_____

Share your group's decision with the rest of the class. Answer any questions, and defend your group's solution.

Putting It All Together

Giving an Oral Presentation

In a three-minute presentation, share with your class interesting information from your interview with someone who has traveled internationally. Use your notes to help you remember the main points and details of your interview, but do not read your notes. After you finish, answer any questions your classmates might have.

Writing a Journal Entry

After each student gives his or her presentation, write down your thoughts, opinions, reactions, and questions in the journal below.

Journal

In small groups, you might want to discuss some of the ideas that you have written in your journal.

3

International Business and Trade

Presentation Strategy: Taking Notes on Outside Reading

Discussion Strategy: Asking Questions in a Group Setting

1. What do you see in the drawing?

2. What products does your country export (sell to other countries)?

3. What products does your country import (buy from other countries)?

Focus Questions

Discuss the following questions.

1. What effect has international trade had on your country?
2. Does international business or trade affect your life now? If so, how?
3. Do you think you will be involved in international business in the future? If so, what type of business?

Background Reading 📼

Read the article about the history of world trade. Then complete the exercise that follows.

> Countries and cultures have been trading with each other for centuries. Before the nineteenth century, world trade was limited because transportation was limited. World trade grew rapidly during the nineteenth century because of the *Industrial Revolution* and the advances in transportation that resulted.
>
> In the early part of the twentieth century, however, serious breakdowns in world trade resulted from two world wars and a world economic depression. During the Great Depression of the 1930s, many countries created trade *barriers* to try to *protect* their industries from *competition*. This "protectionist" policy made the Depression even worse.
>
> After World War II, international trade rapidly increased. Organizations such as the World Bank and the International Monetary Fund were set up right after World War II to encourage international business and trade.
>
> In recent years, free trade agreements between countries have created free trade *zones*. Many economists and political leaders believe that the entire world should become a free trade zone. However, many others are afraid of this idea because they believe that some national industries should be protected from international trade. What do you think?
>
> **Industrial Revolution** The period when societies started moving from being agricultural to being industrial
>
> **depression** a severe slowing of an economy

> **barrier** an obstruction; something that is in the way
> **competition** the act of people or organizations trying to win at something. Businesses compete for customers.
> **zones** an area used for a specific purpose

Class Discussion

Look at the following statements. Then follow the directions indicated.

1. Write some opinions that you have about world trade. Use the beginnings of the following sentences as examples.

> I know many economists think protectionism is bad, but some industries need to be protected because . . . .

> It's not fair when some countries export many things but do not allow many imports . . . .

> Free trade doesn't help my country much because we import cars and planes, and export only fruits and grains . . . .

> Free trade helps everybody because . . . .

2. In small groups, share the opinions you have written down.
3. Discuss the pros and the cons of free trade versus protectionism. Write down ideas that are developed during the discussion. Then share some of your ideas with the entire class.

Presentation Strategy
Taking Notes on Outside Reading

Synthesis Project

It is often necessary to do outside reading in order to get additional information for a presentation. Taking notes is essential when doing outside reading.

1. The article about international trade was brief. To get a deeper understanding of international business and trade, do some outside reading. Choose an area of international business or trade that

interests you. Then go to a library and/or bookstore and find relevant articles from magazines, books, and newspapers to read.

2. When you do outside research on a topic, it is important that you take notes on each article that you read. Your notes should include:

    *   Main points or important ideas;

    *   Points of view or opinions of different authors;

    *   Specific examples that support the author's main points;

    *   Your conclusions about what you read.

If you gather information from several different sources, it will help you organize your notes if you fill out note cards like the one below for each of your sources.

Title:
Author:
Page(s):
Important ideas:

Author's points of view:
Specific examples:

Conclusions:

---

3. Write a summary of each article you read so you can be prepared to give a four-minute oral presentation at the end of this unit. In your summaries, be sure to

    *   use your own words;

    *   present what the authors said accurately;

    *   focus on the major points of the article(s).

4. Be sure to include the following information for each article that you summarize:

- Title of the article

  _____

- Name of the author(s)

  _____

  _____

  _____

- A general statement about the topic

  _____

  _____

  _____

- What the author(s) argues for (pros)

  _____

  _____

  _____

- What the author(s) argues against (cons)

  _____

  _____

  _____

- Important details, facts, or statistics the author(s) write about

  _____

  _____

  _____

- The conclusions of the author(s)

_____

_____

_____

Discussion Strategy
Asking Questions in a Group

When you are discussing a subject in a group, it is important to try to get everyone involved in the discussion. One way to achieve this goal is to ask people information questions about the topic being discussed. Questions that begin with "What," "Where," "Can you tell me," and "How much" are ways to ask for information. For example:

What products does your country export?

Where is the oil-producing section of your country?

Can you tell me what your country imports?

How much rice does your country export?

Another way to involve people in the discussion is to ask for their opinions. It is as important to ask for the opinions of other group members as it is to state your own opinions. Questions that begin with "In your opinion" or "What do you think" are common ways to ask for someone's opinion. For example:

In your opinion, do you think there will be more free trade zones in the future?

What do you think of the trade policies of your country?

In small groups, discuss international trade. Use the information you gathered from your outside reading. Practice asking other group members for information they may have about the topic, and then ask their opinions about the information.

Speaking and Thinking Critically

Reacting to Information

Work with a partner. Take turns asking and answering the following questions. Take notes as your partner speaks. Then share your notes in small groups.

1. In your opinion, is there an industry in your country that should be protected? Why or why not?

_____

_____

_____

2. What do you think your country's international trade policy should be?

_____

_____

_____

3. Can you tell me what countries are your country's most important trading partners?

_____

_____

_____

Discussing Alternatives

Work in groups of four. Read the following information about economic problems in a developing country and the solutions recommended to solve the problems. If you don't like any of the recommendations given, suggest other possibilities.

Case Study

You are part of a committee appointed by the Minister of Trade and Commerce of Derbia. The major mineral exports of the country are tin, zinc, copper, and silver. The major agricultural exports are potatoes, corn, coffee, and wheat. The prices for most of the country's exports have fallen dramatically over the past two years. At the same time, costs of imports such as oil, cars, electrical appliances, and other manufactured goods have risen dramatically. The *trade deficit* and *unemployment* are increasing. The people work hard but they are poorly educated and many of them can't read, so the *illiteracy* rate is high. Your committee must decide what to do and give the Minister some recommendations.

Recommendation 1: Limit imports. Only allow oil and cars to be imported, but import 50 percent fewer cars.

Recommendation 2: Ask international companies to invest money inside the country. Agree not to tax any foreign companies that build factories inside the country for five years if they help train local employees.

Recommendation 3: Communicate with other governments which export the same products, and try to form a *cartel* to increase prices. As a result income earned on exports would increase.

Recommendation 4: Think of your own solution.

trade deficit   the situation that exists when a country buys more than it sells

unemployment   the condition of not having a job; lack of employment

illiteracy   the state of being unable to read or write

cartel   an association formed for the purpose of creating a monopoly (usually by a group of businesses or governments)

Now write down the pros and cons of each recommendation.

Recommendation 1

Pros

_____

_____

_____

Cons

_____

_____

_____

Recommendation 2

Pros

_____

_____

_____

Cons

_____

_____

_____

Recommendation 3

Pros

_____

_____

_____

Cons

_____

_____

_____

Recommendation 4

Pros

_____

_____

_____

Cons

_____

_____

_____

Making a Decision

Consider the pros and cons of each of the recommendations you have discussed in the previous section. Discuss them within your group, and then decide which is the best solution to Derbia's economic problems.

_____

_____

_____

Share your group's decision with the rest of the class. Answer any questions, and defend your group's solution.

Putting It All Together

Giving an Oral Presentation

In a four-minute presentation, share with your class information you obtained from your outside reading. Use your notes and summaries to help you remember the information in the articles you read. After you finish, answer any questions your classmates might have.

Writing a Journal Entry

After each student gives his or her presentation, write down your thoughts, opinions, reactions, and questions in the journal below.

Journal

In small groups, you might want to discuss some of the ideas that you have written in your journal.

U N I T 4

The Environment

Presentation Strategy: Presenting Information Gathered from Outside
Reading

Discussion Strategy: Agreeing and Disagreeing

1. What do you see in the drawing?
2. What are your reactions to what you see?
3. What kind of damage to the environment is being shown in the drawing?
4. Have you ever seen anything like this before? Where?
5. What can be done about this kind of problem?

Discussion Focus

The Environment

Focus Questions

Discuss the following questions.

1. What can individuals do to help the environment?
2. What are some actions that countries can take to help the environment?

Background Reading 📼

Read the following articles about issues related to the environment. Then complete the exercise that follows.

Loss of Rain Forests Continues

Tropical rains forests all around the world are being destroyed at the rate of about 50 million *acres* a year.[1] *Land development*, *mining*, and *logging* are the main causes of the destruction. Thousands of types of insects and animals that are important to the world's *ecosystem* can be found only in rain forests. As the rain forests are destroyed, the ecosystem becomes unbalanced. In addition, most of the world's 250,000 different types of plants are found in rain forests.[2] Important drugs that can help people fight diseases come from these plants. As a result, possible cures for diseases are being lost forever as the rain forests disappear.

acre(s) a measure of land

land development the process of taking land in its natural state and building on it

mining the process of taking natural resources from the land

logging the process of cutting down trees for wood products

ecosystem a community of plants and animals and the environment in which they live

Problem of Acid Rain Grows

Acid rain is rain that has high levels of *acid* caused by air pollution from factories, automobiles, and other sources. Scientists think that acid rain is the main cause of the high levels of acid in 75 percent of the lakes and 47 percent of the streams studied in the United States. Approximately 4 percent of the lakes in the U.S. already have such high levels of acid that almost nothing can live in them. Another 5 percent of the lakes in the U.S. have levels of acid that *threaten* various fish and plants.[3] If nothing is done to control the amount of pollutants in the air, many more lakes and streams will become polluted, resulting in the loss of many types of *aquatic life*.

acid   a chemical containing hydrogen that may destroy things it touches

threaten   endanger

aquatic life   plants or animals that live in water

Five Percent of Ozone Destroyed

Ozone is a layer of gas that surrounds the Earth and protects plant, animal, and human life from harmful *radiation* from the sun. Unfortunately, ozone *depletion* is happening all over the world, particularly in the antarctic and arctic regions.[4] Ozone depletion harms agriculture, and kills aquatic life in the oceans, rivers, and lakes. Chemicals such as CFCs (chlorofluorocarbons), which are found in refrigerators, air conditioners, and *aerosol cans*, destroy ozone. Some scientists estimate that up to 5 percent of the Earth's ozone layer has been destroyed already.[5] Fortunately, fifty-nine countries around the world have agreed to stop making CFCs.[6] In fact, most CFCs will be *banned* by the end of the century. Nevertheless, the ozone continues to disappear, and the danger to life on our planet continues to grow.

radiation   energy that is released from atoms and molecules when they undergo change

depletion   reduction

aerosol cans   containers from which gas under pressure is used to give off a spray

banned   prohibited

Class Discussion

Look at the following statements. Then follow the directions.

1. After you have read the articles about the environment, think of at least two questions related to the news stories.

2. When everyone in the class has two questions in mind, begin a chain of questions. The first speaker should ask the person next to him or her a question. This continues so that each student asks and answers at least one question. Look at the example.

Student A:	Do you know what causes acid rain?
Student B:	Air pollution from cars and factories. Do you think the loss of ozone will harm humans?
Student C:	I'm not sure. I've heard that there may be more cases of skin cancer. What do you think will happen if more rain forests are destroyed?
Student D:	There will be fewer birds and plants. Do you think ...?

Presentation Strategy
Presenting Information Gathered from Outside Reading

Synthesis Project

After you gather information from outside reading, it is important to organize your notes so you can give a well-organized presentation.

1. Choose an environmental issue that interests you. The topic can be one already discussed in this unit, one that will be introduced in the discussion strategy section on page 39, or another topic. Read about the issue in the library and talk about it with English speakers outside of class. Take notes about the important ideas that develop during your reading and conversations, using the note-taking strategies discussed on page 26 in Unit 3.

2. Organize the ideas you gathered from your outside research to prepare a five-minute oral presentation that you will give at the end of this unit. Use the following hints to help you prepare your presentation:

- When making an oral presentation, speak from your notes. If you write your speech out, you will be tempted to read it to the class.
- Look at your audience when you speak. Establish eye contact with classmates.
- Use pictures, charts, and graphs to illustrate your ideas. Such tools are very helpful to the listeners.
- Encourage follow-up discussion of your points.

Discussion Strategy
Agreeing and Disagreeing

When you are having a discussion, it is okay to disagree with someone else's ideas, but it is important to be tactful when you are disagreeing. Being tactful means disagreeing with someone else's ideas without offending or insulting that person. If you use words like *perhaps, maybe, possibly,* and *probably* you will sound polite and reasonable. For example:

> I like your idea, but what about ...

> I agree with many of the things you have said, but perhaps we can look at the problem differently ...

> Maybe there is another way of looking at this issue—for instance, ...

> It's possible that we need to look at this problem in another way ...

It is also good, when you are having a discussion, to point out when you are in agreement with someone. For example:

> I agree with you ...

> I think that's a very good point ...

> I think you're right ...

1. Work with a partner. Read the following controversial statements related to environmental issues. Then discuss other ways of looking at the issues.

a. Recycling (glass, cans, newspaper, plastics) is not economically worth the effort.

> **Student A** I agree that recycling seems expensive now, but maybe we should look at this issue another way: Can we afford not to recycle?

b. The protection of endangered species (types of plants or animals that are in danger of dying out) is the responsibility of government.

> **Student B** I agree with the statement that government has the responsibility to protect endangered animals, but perhaps individuals can do more ...

c. Developed nations have the responsibility to impose (force) environmental protection policies on the entire world.

d. The use of nuclear energy should be encouraged.

e. Farming with chemicals poisons the environment.

f. Electronic communication (computers, fax machines, and copy machines) has not been good from an environmental point of view because it has caused a dramatic increase in the amount of paper being consumed.

2. In small groups, discuss some environmental issues you feel strongly about. Try to be tactful if you disagree with a group member by using some of the words and phrases discussed on page 39.

Speaking and Thinking Critically

Reacting to Information

1. Which environmental problem do you think is the most serious? Write your answer in the space provided.

_____

_____

_____

2. Share your answer with another student. Give reasons why you think this is the most serious environmental problem. Does your partner agree or disagree? Discuss your opinions.

Discussing Alternatives

In small groups, read the following case study, which describes an environmental problem and the solutions recommended to solve the problem. If you don't like any of the recommendations given, suggest other possibilities.

Case Study

In an area of Nemalzia, a developing country, a group of environmentalists is trying to stop land development that is destroying large areas of a rain forest. The environmentalists are saying that many species of plants, insects, and birds found in the rain forest are dying. They are also saying that the rain forest itself is extremely important for the *ecology* of the entire planet. However, land developers and mining company owners say that development is very important for Nemalzia's economy. The trees that are cut down can supply wood for houses and other needs, and minerals such as gold and silver, which lie beneath the forest, can make the country richer. Land developers also state that developing and mining the land has created thousands of jobs. If development of the rain forest is stopped, people will lose their jobs and many families will go hungry.

ecology the study of how plants and animals interact with their environment

Recommendation 1: The government should immediately stop all development. Because this action will benefit everyone worldwide, richer countries should give money to help with the expected loss of income.

Recommendation 2: Allow development to continue, but turn half of the rain forest into a national park where no development is allowed.

> **Recommendation 3:** Allow some development, but slow it down. Turn part of the rain forest over to the travel/tourism industry to encourage preservation of the rain forest.
>
> **Recommendation 4:** Think of your own solution.

Now discuss the pros and cons of each solution. Be sure to take notes during the discussion.

Recommendation 1

Pros

_____

_____

_____

Cons

_____

_____

_____

Recommendation 2

Pros

_____

_____

_____

Cons

_____

_____

_____

Recommendation 3

Pros

_____

_____

_____

Cons

_____

_____

_____

Recommendation 4

Pros

_____

_____

_____

Cons

_____

_____

_____

Making a Decision

Consider the pros and cons of each of the recommendations you have
discussed in the previous section. Consult, agree, and disagree within
your group, and then decide which is the best solution to Nemalzia's
environmental problem.

_____

_____

_____

Share your group's decision with the rest of the class. Answer any questions, and defend your group's solution.

Putting It All Together

Giving an Oral Presentation

1. In a five-minute presentation, share with your class information you obtained from your outside reading. Use the hints on page 39 to help you prepare an appropriate presentation. After you finish, answer any questions your classmates might have.
2. Listen carefully as each of your classmates also gives his or her presentation.
3. Prepare at least one question to ask each speaker as he or she finish the presentation. Remember to be tactful if you don't agree with the speaker's ideas.

Writing a Journal Entry

After each student gives his or her presentation, write down your thoughts, opinions, reactions, and questions in the journal below.

Journal

In small groups, you might want to discuss some of the ideas that you have written in your journal.

Ethnocentrism

Presentation Strategy: Presenting Differing Points of View
Discussion Strategy: Incorporating Differing Points of View

1. What do you see in the drawing?
2. Do you know the meanings of the phrases on the signs?
3. What are your reactions to the signs?

Discussion Focus
Ethnocentrism

Focus Questions

Discuss the following questions.

1. What is ethnocentrism?
2. What causes ethnocentrism?

Background Reading 📼

Read the following article about ethnocentrism. Then complete the exercise that follows.

> What is ethnocentrism? The definition given by Webster's *New World Dictionary* is the following: "The *emotional attitude* that one's own *ethnic* group, nation, or culture is *superior* to all others."[1] Ethnocentrism is a problem in the world today because, unlike centuries ago, people from different ethnic groups come into contact with each other all the time. Ethnocentrism often causes difficulties when people from two different ethnic, national, racial, or religious backgrounds *interact* and the people don't understand each other.
>
> The beginning of ethnocentrism dates back many centuries, to a time when people lived in small groups called tribes. Each tribe was held together by fear of other tribes. This helped bring each tribe together, and allowed it to survive.
>
> Whatever the original causes of ethnocentrism, many think it is a major obstacle to world peace and unity. Ethnocentrism causes feelings of superiority, lack of trust, or misunderstanding all over the world. In extreme cases, ethnocentrism among different groups leads to war. At the very least, it often leads to problems and unhappiness.
>
> **emotional attitude**   very strong feelings about something
>
> **ethnic**   relating to a group of people who are different from other groups by language, customs, and culture

superior	higher in status or rank
interact	actively communicate
obstacle	something in the way

Class Discussion

Discuss the following questions in a small group or with a partner. Take notes about your discussion. Then share your notes with the class.

1. Have you seen or experienced ethnocentric behavior? When? Where?

2. Do you agree that ethnocentrism may have helped solidify individual tribes thousands of years ago? Why or why not? How?

3. Do you agree with the article that ethnocentrism is a major problem in the world today? Why or why not?

4. Look at the drawing on page 46. Are there similar phrases in your language about people working together? If yes, translate them into English and discuss them with your classmates.

Presentation Strategy:
Presenting Differing Points of View

Synthesis Project

When presenting points of view that are different from your own, it is important to keep in mind that people's ideas and opinions are often shaped by their cultural, ethnic, or religious backgrounds.

1. With your teacher and classmates, think of several different issues that are somewhat controversial. Choose one issue that you would like to explore and write down the questions you want to ask. Leave space between the questions so you can take notes. Then interview two or three people whose ethnic backgrounds are different from your own. The people you interview may be your classmates or people from outside the class.

2. When you ask people for interviews, be sure to make polite requests for their time. The following are some ways to request interviews politely:

   a. Do you have a few minutes? Could I please ask you a few questions about ...?

   b. Could I please ask you a few questions about ...? I'm trying to gather information for a class presentation.

   c. I would really appreciate it if I could talk to you about ... .

   d. I'm going to be giving a talk in a class. Would you mind talking to me for a few minutes?

   Also, be sure to tell the people the purpose of your interview. If a person is uncomfortable talking about the topic you have chosen, then thank that person for his or her time and interview someone else. If the person agrees to the interview, but wishes to remain anonymous (name not mentioned), respect that wish.

3. Prepare a five-minute presentation to give at the end of this unit. Choose a point of view that is not your own, and present it objectively to your class. Try to be tolerant of the point of view you chose. Remember that your job is to report what someone else feels or thinks, not your own feelings. Here are some hints:

   a. Focus on the pros of the point of view.

   b. Think about why the person has this point of view.

   c. If necessary, ask some background questions so that you can better understand the person's opinion.

Then answer any questions and defend the position.

Discussion Strategy
Incorporating Different Points of View

When discussing an issue in a group, it is important to consider other people's points of view in order for there to be real communication and exchange of ideas. Remember that different points of view are often shaped by different ethnic, cultural, or religious backgrounds.

1. In small groups, pick another controversial topic, one you are not using for your individual projects. Choose a social, political, or religious topic, or any other issue group members have an opinion about.

2. Have each member share his or her opinions about the topic chosen. Others in the group should listen carefully and take notes, but not argue with the opinions of the speaker, even if they strongly disagree. The listeners should try to do the following:
   a. Give the speaker their full attention by establishing eye contact as he or she speaks.
   b. Act interested in what the speaker is saying.

3. After everyone in the group has given his or her opinion about the topic, study your notes for a few minutes. Is there a pattern to people's opinions? Do people from the same ethnic backgrounds share the same opinions? Do you think that people's ethnic backgrounds affect their thinking on certain topics? Why?

4. Discuss the process of thinking/writing/talking about other points of view with your classmates.

Speaking and Thinking Critically

Reacting to Information

1. In the space on the next page, draw a map of the world from your memory. Do not look at any professional maps. Be sure to include all the continents except Antarctica.

2. In small groups, compare your maps. Discuss the differences. How does your map compare with those of your classmates? What are the differences?

3. Now look at the world map on pages 2 and 3. With your classmates, discuss the maps you drew, and then compare them with the map on pages 2 and 3. Are there any patterns? Is one continent from your classmates' maps usually larger than it should be? Is one continent usually smaller than it should be? Why? Is the area you come from larger or smaller than it should be? Why?

Discussing Alternatives

In small groups, read the following case study about problems between two ethnic groups and the solutions recommended to solve the problems. If you don't like any of the recommendations given, suggest other possibilities.

Case Study

President Kimbura of Zanato is meeting with his *advisors* to discuss the serious ethnic problem that faces their country. There are two ethnic groups in the country, the Zanas and the Toshos. They both want more independence. Fighting between the ethnic groups has increased in recent months.

The larger ethnic group, the Zanas, makes up about 53 percent of the population; the Toshos make up about 47 percent of the population. The Zanas have most of the political power in the country. Not only is the president a Zana, but 73 percent of the members of Congress are also

Zanas because the country is divided by *districts*, and each district elects one representative to Congress. Seventy-three percent of the districts have a Zana majority. The Toshos, on the other hand, are richer. The districts that are populated mainly by Toshos have many natural resources such as gold and diamonds. The large mining companies are controlled by Toshos.

The Zanas want more of the mineral wealth of the country, and the Toshos want more political power. In addition, the Zanas and Tosho have a long history of disliking each other even before Zanato was a country. The only part of the country where Zanas and Toshos live in peace is in the capital city of Tozobia. This *cosmopolitan* city is the main *port* of the country. Here, Zanas and Toshos live and work together; they also frequently intermarry.

The president and most of his advisors don't want to divide the country; they feel that in order for the country to develop and succeed, unity is essential. On the other hand, they want to avoid fighting and some of the advisors feel that the only way to do that is to divide up the country into *autonomous* provinces.

advisors people who give others needed information

district part of a country, state, or city made for a specific purpose such as for voting or for schools

cosmopolitan worldly or sophisticated

port a city or town where ships can load or unload

autonomous self-governing, independent

Recommendation 1: Reserve 50 percent of the seats in Congress for the Zanas and 50 percent for the Toshos. Give the gold and diamond mines to the government to control and share the profits equally between the two groups.

Recommendation 2: Change the voting districts so that more of the districts would have a majority of Toshos. Keep the mines private, but create laws forcing the mining companies to hire more Zanas.

Recommendation 3: Tax the mines at a much higher rate, and spend the money on more social programs for the Zanas. Keep the voting districts and the Congress the same, but change the law so that the president must be a Tosho.

Recommendation 4: Think of your own solution.

Now discuss the pros and cons of each solution. Be sure to take notes during the discussion.

Recommendation 1

Pros

_____

_____

_____

Cons

_____

_____

_____

Recommendation 2

Pros

_____

_____

_____

Cons

_____

_____

_____

Recommendation 3

Pros

_____

_____

_____

Cons

_____

_____

_____

Recommendation 4

Pros

_____

_____

_____

Cons

_____

_____

_____

Making a Decision

Consider the pros and cons of each of the recommendations you have discussed in the previous section. Discuss them within your group, and then decide which is the best solution to Zanato's ethnic problem.

_____

_____

_____

Share your group's decision with the rest of the class. Answer any questions, and defend your group's solution.

Putting It All Together

Giving an Oral Presentation

1. In a five-minute presentation, present a point of view that is not your own on the controversial topic you chose on page 48. Use the hints on page 49 to help you present the point of view objectively. After you finish, answer any questions your classmates might have.

2. Listen carefully as each of your classmates gives his or her own five-minute oral presentation. Be sure to use the listening suggestions on page 50, even if you don't agree with the speaker's opinion.

Writing a Journal Entry

After each student gives his or her presentation, write down your thoughts, opinions, reactions, and questions in the journal below.

Journal

In small groups, you might want to discuss some of the ideas that you have written in your journal.

World Religions

Presentation Strategy: Doing Research for a Presentation

Discussion Strategy: Expressing Feelings and Opinions

1. What are the major religions in your country?
2. What do you consider to be the major religions of the world?

Discussion Focus:
World Religions

Religious Population of the World, by Region: 1991

Religion	Total	Percent distribution	Africa	Asia	Latin America	Northern America	Europe	Soviet Union	Oceania
Total population	5,385,330	100.0	661,803	3,171,511	457,011	277,943	499,544	290,665	26,855
Christians	1,793,660	33.1	317,453	257,926	427,416	237,261	412,790	108,498	22,316
Roman Catholics	1,040,352	18.8	119,244	121,311	397,810	96,315	262,026	5,551	6,095
Protestants	368,209	6.8	84,729	79,969	16,930	95,610	73,766	9,790	7,415
Orthodox	168,683	3.1	27,698	3,587	1,730	5,964	36,080	93,056	568
Anglicans	73,835	1.4	26,063	694	1,275	7,284	32,879	(Z)	5,640
Other Christians	162,581	3.0	59,719	52,365	9,671	32,088	8,039	101	598
Muslims	950,726	17.7	269,959	625,194	11,326	2,642	12,545	38,959	101
Nonreligious[1]	884,468	16.4	1,840	700,523	16,828	25,265	52,289	84,477	3,246
Hindus	719,269	13.4	1,431	714,652	867	1,259	703	2	355
Buddhists	300,127	5.7	20	307,323	530	554	271	404	25
Atheists	236,809	4.4	307	158,429	3,162	1,310	17,563	55,511	527
Chinese folk-religionists	183,646	3.4	12	183,361	71	121	60	1	20
New-religionists	140,778	2.6	20	138,767	61	1,410	50	1	10
Tribal religionists	93,996	1.7	68,484	24,487	918	40	1	–	66
Sikhs	18,461	0.3	26	17,934	8	252	231	1	9
Jews	17,615	0.3	327	5,404	1,071	6,952	1,465	2,220	96
Shamanists	10,302	0.2	1	10,044	1	1	2	252	1
Confucians	5,917	0.1	1	5,883	2	26	2	2	1
Baha'is	5,402	0.1	1,451	2,630	785	363	90	7	76
Jains	3,724	0.1	51	3,649	4	4	15	–	1

continued on page 60

Religious Population of the World, by Region: 1991

Shintoists	3,163	0.1	(Z)	3,160	1	1	1	(Z)	1
Other religionists	18,268	0.3	420	120,651	3,501	482	1,466	330	4

[In thousands, except percent. Refers to adherents of all religions as defined and enumerated for each of the world's countries in *World Christian Encyclopedia* (1982), projected to mid-1991, adjusted for recent data]

– Represents zero

Z Fewer than 500

1 Persons professing no religion, nonbelievers, agnostics, freethinkers, and dereligionized secularists indifferent to all religion

2 Follower of traditional Chinese religion (local deities, ancestor veneration, Confucian ethics, Taoism, etc.).

3 Followers of Asiatic 20th-century New Religions, New Religious movements, radical new crisis religions, and non-Christian syncretistic mass religions

Source: U.S. Bureau of the Census, *Statistical Abstract of the United States*: 1992. (112th edition) Washington, DC, 1992.

Focus Questions

Discuss the following questions.

1. The chart on pages 59–60 shows the number of people who follow different religions. Do any of the statistics surprise you?
2. Which religions had the most followers around the world in 1991?
3. Do you think the statistics are different today? Which ones? Why?

Background Reading 📼

Read the following article, which briefly describes several of the world's religions. Then complete the exercise that follows.

> Religion has been part of the human experience since the beginning of recorded history. It has had a tremendous influence on societies and cultures around the world. There are many religions in the world today. The Baha'i Faith, Buddhism, Christianity, Hinduism, Islam, and Judaism have followers around the world.

One of the newest world religions is the Baha'i Faith. The prophet-founder was Baha'u'llah, who lived from 1817–1892. Baha'i teachings stress the need for eliminating religious and racial prejudice and the importance of world unity.[1]

Buddhism was started by Siddhartha Gautama, who was called the "Buddha" and who lived in northern India from 560 to 480 B.C. Buddhism spread throughout Asia into China, Korea, and Japan. Among its teachings, Buddhism encourages "right speech and right *conduct*."[2]

Christianity is based on the teachings of Jesus Christ. Christ's teachings, found in the New Testament of the Bible, emphasize the following: *salvation*, *compassion*, forgiveness, and *monotheism*.

Hinduism is one of the world's oldest religions. One of the most important of the many Hindu texts is called the *Bhagavad Gita*. Hindus believe in *reincarnation* and the importance of good works[3]. Most Hindus live in India.

Islam was founded by the Prophet Muhammad, who lived on the Arabian peninsula from 570 to 632 A.D. The *fundamental* beliefs of Islam are that God is great, Muhammad is His Prophet and the Koran is a book revealed to Muhammad by God.[4]

Judaism is also one of the oldest world religions. Beliefs include monotheism, respect for good conduct, and faith that the future will be better. The most important work in Judaism is the Torah.[5]

conduct   behavior; how one acts

salvation   being saved

compassion   desire to help those who are suffering

monotheism   belief in one God

reincarnation   the belief that the soul reappears in a new body after death

fundamental   basic; most important

Class Discussion

Discuss the following questions in small groups or with a partner. Take notes about your discussion. Then share your notes with the class.

1. What information can you add to the descriptions of each of the religions discussed in the reading?

2. What new information did you learn from the reading?

3. What beliefs are shared by the religions mentioned in the article?

4. The article states that religion "has had a tremendous influence on societies and cultures around the world." How is this true? In what ways has religion shaped and molded our thoughts and actions?

Presentation Strategy
Doing Research for a Presentation

Synthesis Project

Doing research for a presentation is essential. Your research can include interviewing people and doing outside reading. In addition to library books, you can also find valuable information in magazines and newspapers.

1. Choose one of the religions that you read about or a religion that was not included in the background reading. Research the religion at the library and, if you wish, interview people outside of class for additional information about that religion. You may work in teams for this project, with different team members studying different aspects of the religion. If possible, try to include someone who is a member of the religion on each team.

2. Take notes as you research at the library, using index cards similar to the ones you used in Unit 3. Remember to include important ideas, the authors' points of view, specific examples, and conclusions.

3. Use as many sources as you can, and be sure to write them all down. Think carefully about your sources. As you work, ask yourself the following questions:
   a. Is the person who wrote the article or book (or the person you are interviewing) an expert on this religion?
   b. What sources did he or she use?

c. If the source is a magazine, book, or newspaper, is it believable and reliable?

4. When you finish your research, take all of your notes and put the information into logical order. Decide which information to include and which to omit. Include information that is relevant, important, and interesting and omit information that is not.

5. Prepare an oral presentation to give at the end of this unit. Use index cards to organize your research for your presentation. For example:

Information/opinions about topic from first source:

Information/opinions about topic from second source:

Your own information/opinions about topic:

6. Remember to name your sources when giving your presentation.

Discussion Strategy
Expressing Feelings and Opinions

When discussing a topic that is sensitive or emotional, such as religion, it is important to be able to express your feelings and opinions tactfully. The following are expressions that English speakers often use to say how they feel or what they think about something in a non-threatening way.

- I really feel that ...

- My feeling is that ...

- I have strong feelings about that issue because ...

- My opinion about this topic is that ...

- I think that ...

- I believe that it is ...

In small groups, practice expressing your feelings and opinions. Discuss the following question.

> Since many of the world's religions have teachings that stress compassion and respect for others, why is there so much hostility among people throughout the world?

Speaking and Thinking Critically

Reacting to Information

Work with a partner. Take turns asking and answering the following questions. Take notes as your partner speaks. Then share your notes in small groups.

1. Do you think there will ever be peace and harmony among all the religious groups in the world? Why or why not?

_____

_____

_____

2. Will religion be more important in the future? Why or why not?

_____

_____

_____

3. Is it possible to have an ethical or moral society without religion? Why or why not?

_____

_____

_____

Discussing Alternatives

In small groups, read the following case study which describes a religious conflict and the solutions recommended to solve the problem. If you don't like any of the recommendations given, suggest other possibilities.

Case Study

On the island nation of Pacat, a group of leaders is trying to stop the growing hostility between the two main religious groups on the island before conflict breaks out. Both religions stress the improtance of treating neighbors the way you would want to be treated and treating your enemy with kindness. After much discussion, the leaders decided on three possible solutions to the problem. Their recommendations were:

Recommendation 1: Create strict laws forbidding religious discrimination.

Recommendation 2: Educate children during school hours about both religions, emphasizing the importance of religious tolerance.

Recommendation 3: Meet with the leaders of both religions and discuss ways to promote peace and harmony between the two groups. Then use the ideas that come out of the meeting to stop the hostility.

Recommendation 4: What would you add to their list?

Now discuss the pros and cons of each solution. Be sure to take notes during the discussion.

Recommendation 1

Pros

_____

_____

_____

Cons

_____

_____

_____

Recommendation 2

Pros

_____

_____

_____

Cons

_____

_____

_____

Recommendation 3

Pros

_____

_____

_____

Cons

_____

_____

_____

Recommendation 4

Pros

_____

_____

_____

Cons

_____

_____

_____

Making a Decision

Consider the pros and cons of each of the recommendations you have
discussed in the previous section. Discuss them within your group, and
then decide which is the best solution to Pacat's religious conflict.

_____

_____

_____

Share your group's decision with the rest of the class. Answer any
questions, and defend your group's solution.

Putting It All Together

Giving an Oral Presentation

1. In a five-minute presentation, present information concerning the religion you or your group chose to research. Be sure to present the information in a sensitive, tactful way. If you are working as a team, be sure to allow each member an opportunity to speak. After you finish, answer any questions your classmates might have.

2. Listen carefully as each of your classmates gives his or her own oral presentation.

Writing a Journal Entry

After each student gives his or her presentation, write down your thoughts, opinions, reactions, and questions in the journal below.

Journal

In small groups, you might want to discuss some of the ideas that you have written in your journal.

U N I T **7**

World Organizations

Presentation Strategy: Persuading Your Audience

Discussion Strategy: Persuasion

1. What comes into your mind when you think of the term "world organization?"

2. Look at the drawing. Describe what you see.

3. What other world-wide organizations do you know of?

Discussion Focus:
World Organizations

Assistance Rendered by Who in 1986-1987, by Sector and Region
(in $000 US dollars)

SECTOR	Global and interregional activities	Africa	The Americas	South-East Asia	Europe	Eastern Mediterranean	Western Pacific	Total
				REGION				
Direction, coordination and managament	34,632	10,318	2,364	23,462	6,773	7,155	2,807	65,397
Health system infrrastructure	28,092	53,845	25,529	29,409	8,100	28,785	25,047	198,928
Health science and technology-health promotion and care	93,893	21,898	28,320	27,896	11,412	20,908	26,331	230,666
Health science and technology-disease provention and control	115,340	83,291	15,618	27,432	2,185	16,282	17,193	277,345
Program support	93,605	17,344	8,235	4,893	14,383	7,507	6,074	277,345
Total	365,562	80,698	80,075	92,037	41,913	80,639	77,453	924,381

Adapted from *The Yearbook of the United Nations*, 1987, Volume 41, page 1226.
Reproduced with permission.

Focus Questions

Discuss the following questions.

1. Look at the chart above. It shows the amount, in dollars, spent by the World Health Organization during one year. Which region of the world received the most money?
2. What sector received the most money?
3. Do you think more money is spent on health now? Why or why not?

Background Reading 📼

The following article is about two world organizations that were created in the twentieth century to bring about peace and order in the world: the League of Nations, organized after World War I, and the United Nations, established after World War II.[1] Read the article. Then complete the exercise that follows.

The League of Nations was the first attempt by political leaders to form a world organization to *promote* international peace and cooperation. The attempt failed when war broke out in the 1930s and 1940s. The League of Nations did, however, accomplish some important goals. Because of its work, the health and well-being of people in many countries were improved and action was taken to fight illegal drugs. The League of Nations was officially *terminated* on April 18, 1946, to make way for the United Nations.[2]

The United Nations (U.N.) was officially formed on October 24, 1945. Its goals are to promote peace and friendly relations among nations and to *address* the many humanitarian, social, and economic challenges that face us all. The United Nations has six major agencies: the Security Council, the General Assembly, the Economic and Social Council, the Trusteeship Council, the Secretariat, and the International Court of Justice. In addition, the U.N. has formed many special agencies to address more specific problems. The World Health Organization (WHO), for example, was formed to improve health throughout the world. The World Bank and the International Monetary Fund (IMF) were founded to finance economic development projects, and the General Agreement on Tariffs and Trade (GATT) was formed to promote and *regulate* international trade.[3]

promote   support or encourage something

terminate   end something

address   direct energy and resources towards a goal

regulate   guide or manage

Class Discussion

Discuss the following questions in small groups or with a partner. Take notes on your discussion. Then share your notes with the class.

1. The article points out that the League of Nations was an important first step towards promoting world peace. Do you agree? Why or why not?

2. What special agency of the United Nations do you think is the most interesting? Why?

3. Have you ever considered working at the United Nations? In what way?

4. Do you think the United Nations should become more involved in military conflicts around the world? Why or why not?

5. Do you feel that present-day world organizations are effective? How can they be made more effective?

Presentation Strategy
Persuading your Audience

Persuasion is an important aspect of communication. To persuade means to win someone over to your point of view. It involves desiring, and trying to get, a certain response from your audience. In this section, you will try to convince (persuade) your audience that your judgment about a world organization is a correct one.

Synthesis Project

1. Read about a world organization or agency of interest to you. Choose one of the agencies of the United Nations mentioned in the article, or choose a different world organization. You can choose an international organization that relates to sports, the environment, travel, business, or politics.

2. As you do your background reading, take notes you can use to prepare an oral presentation to give at the end of this unit. Be sure to

include information you can give the class to persuade them that this organization plays an important role in world affairs.

3. Practice trying to persuade a friend, classmate, or family member that your point of view on the topic is a good one.

Discussion Strategy
Persuasion

1. When you persuade your audience in a discussion, it is important that you try not to be combative (ready to fight). Try to understand other points of view. If you are successful in developing a trusting relationship with the people with whom you are talking, you will discover that they are much more likely to be open to your ideas. It is also important to keep in mind the following points:

    a. You must establish credibility or believability with the audience, so the audience will consider you a reliable source. You are considered reliable if you are knowledgeable on all sides of the issue. One of the ways to become knowledgeable is to do a lot of reading on your topic.

    b. Show enthusiasm about your topic. Your audience will be more interested if they see your enthusiasm.

    c. Try to create a trusting relationship with the audience. You can do this by being open, friendly, and honest.

    d. Make sure that the facts you present are true and that your conclusions are based on the facts you give.

    e. Present your topic in a logical sequence.

    f. Don't be combative or threatening because this will only put your audience on the defensive.

    g. State the other side of the argument clearly so that your audience will understand that you have looked at the options.

2. Look back to the chart on page 71. In your opinion, which region of the world should receive the most money and assistance from the World Health Organization today? Now try to justify your opinion by persuading a partner that your opinion is a good one. Keep in mind the

points about persuasion listed earlier in this section. Following are some additional hints to help you persuade an audience to agree with you:

- Be a good listener. Listen to others' points of view.
- Be willing to make changes in your point of view based on new information.

Speaking and Thinking Critically

Reacting to Information

Work with a partner. Take turns asking and answer the following questions. Take notes as your partner speaks. Then share your notes in small groups.

1. Do you think there will ever be a world government? Why or why not?

_____

_____

2. Do you think there is a need for a world military force, independent of any one country, to enforce peace and order globally? Why or why not?

_____

_____

Discussing Alternatives

Work in groups of five. A group of international leaders has recommended two ways to set up a world government. You are a member of a small panel of leaders chosen to propose a third option. First, read the two recommendations below. Then write a third option. Your option could be to recommend *no* world government.

Recommendation 1: The world government would be made up of two organizations: a world congress and a world court.

A world congress

Each country in the world would elect one representative (individual approved to speak for others) to the congress. Each representative would have one vote. In other words, each country would have one vote.

A world court

The world court would be made up of twenty people who are experts in international law. They would be elected by the world congress to five-year terms. The congress could not elect its own members to the court.

Recommendation 2: The world government would be made up of three organizations: a world congress, a world executive branch (responsible for execution or carrying out the law and concerns of the people it governs), and a panel of scholars.

A world congress

Each country would send representatives to the world congress. The number of members chosen by each country would depend on the size of the population. For example, if a country has 100 million people, it would elect ten representatives; if a country has 10 million people or less, it would elect one representative, and so on.

A world executive branch

Members of a world executive branch would be elected to five-year terms according to the following criteria:

a. Each country would elect one person (a delegate) to attend an international convention.

b. At the convention each delegate would vote for ten people he or she feels should be elected to the executive branch. (The delegate is free to vote for anyone over the age of 30.)

c. The ten people with the most votes (not necessarily a majority of votes) are elected to the executive branch.

A panel of scholars

A panel of scholars would be experts in international law chosen by the executive branch and approved by the congress. The scholars would give advice to the executive branch and to congress, but they would have no power to make laws.

Recommendation 3: Think of your own option.

Now discuss the pros and cons of each option. Be sure to take notes during the discussion.

Recommendation 1

Pros

_____

_____

_____

Cons

_____

_____

_____

Recommendation 2

Pros

_____

_____

_____

Cons

_____

_____

_____

Recommendation 3

Pros

_____

_____

_____

Cons

_____

_____

_____

Making a Decision

Consider the pros and cons of each of the recommendations you have discussed in the previous section. Discuss them within your group, and then decide which is the best option.

_____

_____

_____

Share your group's decision with the rest of the class. Answer any questions, and defend your group's option.

Putting It All Together

Giving an Oral Presentation

1. Be sure to review the points given in this unit about persuasion before giving your presentation.
2. Listen carefully as each of your classmates gives his or her presentation.
3. After each presentation, discuss any changes in point of view you have after listening to the presentation. Discuss how the speaker persuaded you.

Writing a Journal Entry

After each student gives his or her presentation, write down your thoughts, opinions, reactions, and questions in the journal below.

Journal

In small groups, you might want to discuss some of the ideas that you have written in your journal.

8

International Law

Presentation Strategy: Asking Questions during a Presentation

Discussion Strategy: Brainstorming for Ideas

1. Describe what you see in the drawing.
2. Have you ever been in a court of law? Where? When? Why?

Discussion Focus

International Law

Focus Questions

Discuss the following questions.

1. What is international law? Do you know any international laws?
2. How do international laws affect our daily lives?

Background Reading 📼

Read the following article about international law. Then complete the exercise that follows.

What is International Law?

International law refers to the body of rules that is used to control relations among countries. International laws regulate boundaries, the oceans, trade, human rights, foreign *investment* and various other international activities.[1]

History of International Law

International laws began thousands of years ago. Greece and Rome had *treaties* with each other, and in the region of *Mesopotamia*, there were formal agreements among different cultures.[2] In the past century or so, international law has really changed. Over the last fifty years especially, international law has expanded to cover such areas as outer space and deep-sea mining.[3]

Examples of International Law

There are many international laws. For example, the "Law of the Sea" governs the use of international waters.[4] The

"International Law of Outer Space" governs the rights and responsibilities of countries in their use of *satellites*, rockets, and other objects they send into space.[5]

International Court of Justice

The highest court for international law is called the International Court of Justice. Founded by the United Nations in 1945, the International Court of Justice is located in The Hague, Netherlands. There are fifteen judges on the court, one-third (five) of whom are elected every three years to a nine-year term. In order for a judge to be elected to the Court, he or she must receive a majority vote in both the Security Council and the General Assembly of the United Nations. More than one judge cannot be elected from any one country. No government can be forced to go before the Court. In other words, individual governments have to agree that they will *abide* by the decisions of the Court.[6]

investment   money spent on something of value

treaties   formal written agreements among two or more nations

Mesopotamia   area which is now Iraq

satellite   object that orbits (circles) the Earth

abide   obey or submit to

Class Discussion

Discuss the following questions in small groups or with a partner. Take notes on your discussion. Then share your notes with the class.

1. The article says that in the last fifty years international law has changed in many ways. Do you think international law will continue to change? Why? How? In what areas?

2. Only one judge from each country is allowed on the International Court of Justice. Do you think this is a good rule? Why or why not?

3. No government can be forced to go before the International Court of Justice. Do you think this is a good idea? Why or why not?

Presentation Strategy
Asking Questions during a Presentation

Synthesis Project

An oral presentation can stimulate interesting discussion about the topic presented. To encourage your listeners to discuss the topic you present, invite them to ask questions during or after your presentation.

1. Choose an area of international law that is of interest to you and research it at the library. Ask the librarian to help you find sources for the topic you choose. You may also want to talk to local organizations, such as environmental groups or businesses, who know about specific areas of international law. Some suggested areas to research are laws related to international trade and business, nuclear weapons testing, environmental laws, international travel, human rights, and the laws of the sea or space.

2. From your research on the topic you choose, prepare an oral presentation to give at the end of this unit.

3. At the end of your presentation, think about asking your audience questions in order to encourage discussion. To do this you can tell the audience that the formal part of your presentation is over, using such phrases as "that concludes my presentation," or "that ends my talk on ...," or another phrase you are comfortable with. Then invite questions from the audience. Following are examples of what you could say:
   a. Are there any questions?
   b. I'd be happy to answer any questions you have.
   c. Does anyone have a question?
   d. Please feel free to ask any questions you might have.
   e. Are there any comments or questions?

4. Answer any questions the audience has. Encourage as much discussion as possible.

Note: If you do not know the answer to a question, do not pretend that you do. Be honest with your audience. Let them know that you will try to find out the answer if you do not know it now. Then, get back to them with the answer as soon as you can.

Discussion Strategy

Brainstorming for Ideas

Sometimes, during a question and answer period after a presentation, an unusual issue or problem may be brought up for which no one has a solution. One way to solve problems in a group is by brainstorming. Brainstorming is a method for solving problems. To brainstorm, each person in a group offers as many solutions as he or she can think of to a problem. When you brainstorm, you need to put aside "reality" for a while, and just say what comes to your mind.

The following dialogue is an example of three people brainstorming to come up with a possible solution to the problem of pollution in the oceans.

Hiromasa	I feel terrible about what has happened to the oceans. They are so polluted now.
Susan	We should really do something. Let's brainstorm some possible solutions.
Phillipe	OK. We could get some nets and start taking some of the garbage out ourselves.
Hiromasa	That's a good thought, but I think the problem is way too large for that approach.
Susan	We could start a petition to get the United Nations to force countries to stop dumping garbage into the oceans.
Hiromasa	We could also start writing articles to newspapers.
Susan	We could get volunteers to watch out for people who dump garbage and chemicals into the oceans.
Hiromasa	How about calling a television station so we can get news coverage?
Phillipe	We could ...

1. In small groups, brainstorm for ideas to address the following issue:

   Many people, organizations, and governments break international laws without being punished. Come up with ways to strengthen enforcement of international laws. List the ideas in the space provided.

_____

_____

_____

2. Discuss your ideas and decide which one(s) make sense. Then share your ideas with the rest of the class.

Speaking and Thinking Critically

Reacting to Information

Work with a partner. Take turns asking and answering the following questions. Take notes as your partner speaks. Then share your notes in small groups.

1. If you could write one international law, what would it be?

_____

_____

_____

2. What area(s) of international law do you think world leaders should be working on now?

_____

_____

_____

Discussing Alternatives

In small groups, read the following case study, which describes a problem relating to international law. Brainstorm for ideas to solve the legal problem described. Try to be as objective as you can.

Case Study

Carlisma shares a long border with Tanubia. Carlisma is a developed country with a lot of industry and wealth. Tanubia is a poor country with little industry but a large population. In recent years, many people from Tanubia have been entering Carlisma illegally to get jobs. Leaders of Carlisma have decided to consult with leaders of Tanubia to come up with a solution to the problem of illegal migration.

Recommendation 1: The Carlisman government should write a new law that would imprison, for two years, any noncitizen found working in Carlisma.

Recommendation 2: The Carlisman government should try to persuade the Tanubian government to change its law concerning outside investment, so it is easier for Carlisman businesses to be in Tanubia. Carlisman businesses could then hire Tanubian workers in Tanubia.

Recommendation 3: Think of your own idea.

Now discuss the pros and cons of each solution. Be sure to take notes during the discussion.

Recommendation 1

Pros

_____

_____

_____

Cons

_____

_____

_____

Recommendation 2

Pros

_____

_____

_____

Cons

_____

_____

_____

Recommendation 3

Pros

_____

_____

_____

Cons

_____

_____

_____

Making a Decision

Consider the pros and cons of each of the recommendations you have
discussed in the previous section. Consult, agree, and disagree within
your group, and then decide which is the best solution to Carlisma's and
Tanubia's problem.

_____

_____

_____

Share your group's decision with the rest of the class. Answer any
questions, and defend your group's solution.

Putting It All Together

Giving an Oral Presentation

1. In a five-minute presentation, share with your class information you
   obtained from your outside research on an area of international law.
   After your presentation, encourage your classmates to ask questions.
   Then try to answer their questions. If any specific problems emerge
   from your discussion, brainstorm with your classmates for possible
   solutions.

2. Listen carefully as each of your classmates gives his or her own
   presentation on an area of international law. As each presentation is
   given, think of a question or two to ask the speaker when he or she
   finishes the presentation. Write the question(s) below.

_____

_____

_____

Writing a Journal Entry

After each student gives his or her presentation, write down your thoughts, opinions, and reactions in the journal below.

Journal

In small groups, you might want to discuss some of the ideas that you have written in your journal.

U N I T **9**

International Education

Presentation Strategy: Listening and Responding to an Audience

Discussion Strategy: Active Listening in a Discussion

1. What do you see in the drawing?
2. Describe the educational system in your country.
3. How do educational systems differ in countries you know about?

Discussion Focus:
International Education

Proficiency Test Scores In Mathematics and Science for 13 Year-Old Students, by Selected Countries: 1991

Area	Average days of instruction per year	Mathematics[1]					Science[2]				
		Rank	Percent correct	Average minutes of mathematics instruction each week	Percent of students who spend 2 hours or more on homework per day	Percent of students who watch television 5 hours or more per day	Rank	Percent correct	Average minutes of mathematics instruction each week	Percent of students who spend 2 hours or more on homework per day	Percent of students who watch television 5 hours or more per day
Canada	188	9	62	226	27	14	9	69	156	26	15
France	174	6	64	230	55	5	10	69	174	55	4
Hungary	177	5	68	106	58	13	4	73	207	61	16
Ireland	173	11	61	189	63	9	14	63	159	66	9
Israel[3]	215	8	63	205	50	20	8	70	181	49	20
Italy[4]	204	7	64	210	79	5	7	70	138	56	5
Jordan	191	15	40	100	56	7	15	57	150	54	10
Scotland	191	10	61	210	14	24	11	69	179	15	23
Slovenia	190	12	57	188	29	4	6	70	283	27	5
South Korea	222	1	73	179	41	11	1	78	144	38	10
Soviet republics	198	4	70	258	52	17	5	71	387	52	19
Spain[6]	100	13	55	235	54	10	12	68	189	62	11

continued on page 93

Proficiency Test Scores In Mathematics and Science for 13 Year-Old Students, by Selected Countries: 1991

Area	Average days of instruction per year	Mathematics[1]					Science[2]				
		Rank	Percent correct	Average minutes of mathematics instruction each week	Percent of students who spend 2 hours or more on homework per day	Percent of students who watch television 5 hours or more per day	Rank	Percent correct	Average minutes of mathematics instruction each week	Percent of students who spend 2 hours or more on homework per day	Percent of students who watch television 5 hours or more per day
Switzerland	207	3	71	251	20	7	3	74	152	21	7
Taiwan	222	2	73	204	44	10	2	76	245	44	7
United States	178	14	55	228	29	20	13	67	233	31	22

1 Includes 75 questions on numbers and operations, measurement, dgeometry, data analysis, statistics, and probability, and algebra and functions.

2 Includes 64 quesitons on life, physical earth and space sciences, and nature of science

3 Hebrew-speaking schools only

4 Emilia-Romagna province only

5 Russian-speaking schools, 14 out of 15 republics only

6 Spanish-speaking schools, Cataluna excluded

7 7out of 26 Cantons only

Source: National Center of Education Statistics, U.S. Department of Education, and the National Science Foundation, *Learning Mathematics and Learning Science*, Feburary 1992

Discuss the following questions.

1. The chart on page 92 and above shows a comparative study done in 1991. What conclusions can you draw from the study?

2. What conclusions can you draw from the chart about the effects of television on performance in school?

3. If the same study were done today, what differences do you think there would be?

Background Reading 📼

Read the following article about international education. Then complete the exercise that follows.

What is international education? If you are studying in another country, you are involved in international education. International education is a term that is used to describe the following areas:

✧ Educational exchanges, in which students from country A study in country B, and students from country B study in country A.

✧ Comparative education, the study of different educational systems in different countries.

✧ Development education, which relates to how education can help developing countries.

✧ Cross-cultural education, which deals with intercultural and international understanding.[1]

International education has been growing in importance for several decades. The number of students who choose to study in foreign countries continues to grow. Recently, for instance, over 400,000 international students from 193 countries were studying in the United States.[2] The Canadian Bureau for International Education estimates that up to 85,000 international students were studying in Canada.[3] In addition, the number of American students seeking advanced business degrees in Europe has been growing.[4] Because of their numbers, international students have provided, and will continue to provide, an important way to promote international understanding and good will.

Class Discussion

Discuss the following questions in small groups or with a partner. Take notes on your discussion. Then share your notes with the class.

1. In your opinion, what are the reasons that large numbers of students study in foreign countries?
2. What do you think is the most important area in international education? Why?
3. How can international education promote international understanding?

Presentation Strategy
Listening and Responding to an Audience

Synthesis Project

When giving a presentation, it is important that you listen to your audience carefully when they ask questions or make comments, so that you are able to respond in an informative way.

1. Interview two or three international students who are not in your class. Find out the following:
   a. Why are they studying in a foreign country?
   b. What are their educational goals?
   c. What do they like and dislike about studying in a foreign country?
   d. What do they think is the most difficult aspect of studying in a foreign country?
   e. What is the biggest difference between the educational systems in their native countries and the country in which they are studying now? For example, is the biggest difference in the curriculum, in the focus on memorizing versus creative thinking, in behavior in the classroom, in teacher/student relationships?
   f. Add your own questions.
2. Using the information from your interviews, prepare a short oral presentation to give at the end of this unit.

3. Be prepared for questions and comments your audience might have. For example, if the people you interviewed said that they had trouble adjusting to the food in their new countries, your audience will also probably comment about the kinds of problems they have had with the food. To encourage further discussion, ask them questions related to their questions and comments.

4. During the discussion period after your presentation, listen carefully to your audience. If someone asks a question, respond to the best of your ability. If you don't know the answer to a question, say that you don't know but that you'll find out. It's also okay to allow other people in the audience to answer a question. The more people participate, the better. In fact, if someone makes a comment instead of asking a question, invite reaction from other people in the audience, or state your own feelings about the comment.

Following are some tips to help you listen and respond to an audience.

Do:
   a. Ask for questions and comments in a friendly and enthusiastic manner.
   b. Encourage discussion by allowing others to respond to questions and comments.
   c. Politely but firmly bring the discussion back to the subject if the discussion goes off the topic.
   d. Give as many people as possible a chance to speak.

Do not:
   a. Get defensive or angry about a question or comment.
   b. Allow one or two people to dominate the discussion.
   c. Allow people to interrupt someone who is speaking.

Discussion Strategy
Active Listening in a Discussion

When you participate in a discussion, it is important to be an active listener. This means asking questions, being attentive, and being interested in (although not necessarily in agreement with) what the speaker says.

1. In small groups, share any international learning experiences you have had. Discuss what impact you think widespread international education will have on your future or the future of your children.

2. During the discussion, allow each group member approximately three minutes to talk. Take notes as each group member speaks. Listen closely as the speaker shares his or her experiences with you. Ask questions to make sure that you understand what the speaker wants to say. For example:

   Speaker A   Were you homesick in the beginning?

   Speaker B   So you had culture shock, right?

3. After everyone in the group has shared his or her opinions and experiences on international education, take a few minutes to study your notes.

4. Present some of your group members' opinions, feelings, and experiences to the rest of the class. Remember to report other people's opinions fairly and tactfully, even if you don't agree with them.

5. Discuss the general themes that emerge. For example, did many students share certain difficulties? Did many students have similar positive experiences? What advice could you give to other people based on what you have learned?

Speaking and Thinking Critically

Reacting to Information

Work with a partner. Take turns asking and answering the following questions. Take notes as your partner speaks. Then share your notes in a small group.

1. If you had the power to make *one* course a requirement for all high school students around the world, what course would you choose? Why?

_____

_____

_____

2. In the future, do you think there will be more or fewer students who study abroad? Why?

_____

_____

_____

Discussing Alternatives

Work in groups of five.

Case Study

You are part of a school committee in a country called Sajuto. Your job is to come up with a curriculum for grades eleven and twelve that will meet the needs of high school students in Sajuto. In the past, most people in Sajuto were farmers. However, in recent years many people have moved from rural areas to the cities to get jobs in factories. Many of the young people in the cities are unemployed because they have few skills.

The school committee's job is to decide upon a curriculum that will prepare the young people of Sajuto for the twenty-first century. So far, the committee has come up with the following list of possible courses:

Accounting	English Literature	Physics
Agriculture	Ethic	Psychology
Algebra	Environmental Studies	Reading (English)
Art Appreciation	Gardening	Sajutese Language
Biology	Geography	Word Processing
Carpentry	Geology	World History
Chemistry	Geometry	World Religions
Computers	Government	Writing (English)
Cooking	Music Theory	Typing
Drafting	National History	World Literature
Economics	Physical Education	

Discuss the different courses, and then decide which ones students should take in grades eleven and twelve. Since there are two semesters in each grade, decide which courses students should take for each semester. Write your choices in the spaces provided. The courses you choose do not have to be from the list. You can add your own choices. Now discuss the pros and cons of your curriculum. Be sure to take notes during the discussion.

Recommendations for Grade Eleven	First Semester	Second Semester

Recommendations for Grade Twelve	First Semester	Second Semester

Recommendation

Pros

_____

_____

_____

Cons

_____

_____

_____

Making a Decision

Consider the pros and cons of the curriculum your group has decided upon. Consult, agree, and disagree within your group, and then decide what is the best curriculum possible.

_____

_____

_____

Share your group's final curriculum with the rest of the class. Explain why you decided on the courses you chose. Answer any questions and defend your group's curriculum.

Putting It All Together

Giving an Oral Presentation

1. In a five-minute presentation, share with your class the information you obtained from your interviews with international students. Remember to ask for questions from your audience.

2. Listen carefully as each of your classmates presents the information obtained from his or her outside interviews. After each presentation, ask questions and share with the speaker your own experiences as an international student.

Writing a Journal Entry

After each student gives his or her presentation, write down your thoughts, opinions, reactions, and questions in the journal below.

Journal

In small groups, you might want to discuss some of the ideas that you have written in your journal.

U N I T **10**

The Future

Presentation Strategy: Controlling the Question and Answer Period

Discussion Strategy: Taking Turns

1. What comes to your mind when you look at the drawing?
2. Do you think you will travel to other planets someday in the future?
    Would you want to? Why or why not?

Discussion Focus

The Future

Focus Questions

Discuss the following questions.

1. What are your thoughts about the future of this planet?
2. What do you worry about when you think about the future?

Background Reading 📼

Read the following article about the future. Then complete the exercise that follows.

> Futurists are people who specialize in predicting the future. According to futurists, the world will be a much different place in the future than it is today. Food, transportation, and medicine will all change dramatically.
>
> For example, the way we grow our food will change. Crops will no longer be protected by harmful *pesticides*, but by natural means such as insects that eat other insects. There will be more *genetically engineered* fruits and vegetables. There will also be an increased number of fish farms to meet the nutritional needs of a growing population.[1]
>
> Major changes in transportation will also be evident. For example, high-speed trains will become more important in the future.[2] More *solar-powered* cars will also be in use. Perhaps ordinary cars will be able to fly and ordinary airplanes will be able to go into outer space.
>
> In the future, futurists predict, people will become more involved in their own health care. The computer will play an increasingly important role in medicine. For example, you will be able to choose a doctor and even perform self-treatment with help from computer software. In the future, *nutrition* and *herbal medicine* will also play much more important roles in the fight against diseases.[3]
>
> **pesticides**   chemicals used for killing insects

> **genetically engineered** changed genetically (Genes are the parts of a cell that determine what a plant or animal will look like.)
>
> **solar powered** powered from the sun
>
> **nutrition** the science of food and diet
>
> **herbal medicine** the use of plants for healing

Class Discussion

Discuss the following questions in small groups or with a partner. Take notes about the discussion. Then share your notes with the class.

1. Do you look forward to eating more genetically engineered fruit and vegetables? How do you think they will be different?

2. Do you think the development of flying cars and commercial airliners that go into space is possible? What other types of transportation do you think you will see in the future?

3. Futurists think that herbal medicine will play a more important role in the future. Have you ever used herbal medicines? Are they commonly used in your country? Which ones? For what purposes?

Presentation Strategy
Controlling the Question and Answer Period

Synthesis Project

During a question and answer period of a presentation, the presenter is responsible for controlling the discussion.

1. Choose a specific area of the future that interests you. For example, you might want to study the future of transportation, medicine, or space exploration. Interview several English speakers outside of your class to understand their views on your topic. Do some outside reading to see what futurists say about the area you have chosen.

2. After you have gathered viewpoints from your outside reading and interviews, prepare an oral presentation to give at the end of this unit.

Keep in mind that, sometimes, problems arise during the discussion period that follows a talk. Think about the following common problems and their solutions as you prepare for your presentation:

Problem 1: Getting people to talk.

> **Solution:** Direct your questions to one member of the audience instead of to the entire audience. For instance, ask one student:
>
> > What do you think?
> >
> > Do you have any questions?
> >
> > What has your experience been ...?
> >
> > Have you ever ...?
> >
> > Could you please share your thoughts with us?
>
> If you still don't get a response, ask other members of the audience questions.

Problem 2: One or two people do all the talking and everyone else remains silent.

> **Solution:** Thank the one or two members of the audience doing most of the talking for their participation, and then politely but firmly say one of the following:
>
> > Let's hear what other people think.
> >
> > Maybe we can get some other opinions.
> >
> > I'd like to give other people in the audience a chance to share their feelings/opinions.
>
> Then direct questions such as the ones suggested for Problem 1 to the people who are silent.

Problem 3: The discussion goes off the topic.

> **Solution:** Politely but firmly remind the audience what the topic is. For instance, if the topic is the future of international trade, and people are talking about the weather, you could say:

Interesting, but what about the trade relationship?

I'd like to get back to the topic if we could.

I don't think that relates to the topic.

Excuse me, let's get back to the topic.

Problem 4: Two or more people talk at the same time.

Solution: Take control of the discussion and allow only one person at a time to speak. It is important to do this politely but firmly. The following statements are examples of what you might say:

Why don't you go first, Roberto? Then Johann can speak next.

Please, one person at a time.

3. Before you give your presentation, practice controlling the question and answer period with a small group of classmates. Use your presentation topic for this practice. Instruct your group to make the question and answer period difficult by acting out some of the problems just discussed. Then practice regaining control of the discussion by using some of the solutions suggested in this section.

Discussion Strategy

Taking Turns

During a discussion, it is not considered polite for one or two people to dominate the conversation. It is important that everyone feel included in the discussion. That way, the discussion will be more meaningful and more information can be introduced. When you are the speaker, it is up to you to control the discussion and the question and answer period that follows it. Following are some examples of polite remarks you can use to suggest that your audience take turns. Read these sentences and practice them when discussing the questions that follow.

Let's have one person at a time speak ...

Let's listen to what Rafael has to say ...

Let's allow some other people a chance to speak ...

It's your turn, Junko ...

Could I say something, please ...

I'd like to say something, please ...

You're next ...

1. In small groups, discuss the following questions. Use the sentences
   just given to help you control the direction of or break into the
   discussion. Take turns controlling the discussion.

   a. What type of work do you plan to do in the future? How might the
      job be different in the future than it is now?

   b. What advice would you give someone who is trying to prepare for
      this type of job?

   c. The study of foreign languages will probably become increasingly
      popular. What other subjects do you think will become more
      popular in school?

   d. What do you think will be the most important health issue in the
      future? Why?

   e. How will computers change our homes in the future?

Speaking and Thinking Critically

Reacting to Information

Work with a partner. Take turns asking and answering the following
questions. Take notes as your partner speaks. Then share your notes in
small groups.

1. Which sports do you think will be the most popular in the future? Why? Which sports will lose their popularity? Why?

_____

_____

_____

2. Do you think there will be world peace in the future? Why or why not?

_____

_____

_____

Discussing Alternatives

Work in small groups. Read the following case study about a sports organization and the strategies it recommends to solve a problem in the future. If you don't like any of the recommendations given, suggest other possibilities.

Case Study

A group of businesspeople is starting a world sports organization, called the Global Basketball League, whose goal is to have basketball replace football (soccer) as the world's most popular sport. The league's plan for the future is to have at least two teams in every country of the world by the year 2010. The Global Basketball League's most difficult problem is promoting basketball in areas of the world where it is not widely known or popular. In order to promote basketball in these areas, the Global Basketball League has come up with the following strategies:

Recommendation 1: Advertise basketball on television and radio. Also, produce a television show about the history of basketball and how it is played.

Recommendation 2: Have star basketball players visit a variety of countries and play exhibition games in all of them.

Recommendation 3: Have coaches and players teach basketball in high schools and colleges in different countries to create interest in the sport.

Recommendation 4: Think of your own strategy.

Now discuss the pros and cons of each strategy. Be sure to take notes during the discussion.

Recommendation 1

Pros

_____

_____

_____

Cons

_____

_____

_____

Recommendation 2

Pros

_____

_____

_____

Cons

_____

_____

_____

Recommendation 3

Pros

_____

_____

_____

Cons

_____

_____

_____

Recommendation 4

Pros

_____

_____

_____

Cons

_____

_____

_____

Making a Decision

Consider the pros and cons of each of the recommendations you have
discussed in the previous section. Discuss them within your group and
then decide which is the best strategy for the Global Basketball League.

_____

_____

_____

Share your group's decision with the rest of the class. Answer any questions and defend your group's strategy.

Putting It All Together

Giving an Oral Presentation

1. Give a brief oral presentation to the class to present the information you gathered from your research on page 105. Lead a class discussion about your topic. Look back at the suggestions for controlling the question and answer period before you give your presentation. Remember to encourage your audience to take turns speaking during the discussion.

2. Listen carefully as each of your classmates gives his or her presentation. As each presentation is given, think of a question or two to ask the speaker. This time, however, test the speaker during the discussion period that follows the presentation. Be a difficult audience:

> Don't ask questions right away;
>
> Several speak at the same time;
>
> Change the topic more than once.

Do not be too difficult; after all, this is just practice. You certainly don't want to give your classmates too hard of a time!

Writing a Journal Entry

After each student gives his or her presentation, write down your thoughts, opinions, and reactions in the journal below.

Journal

_____

_____

_____

_____

_____

_____

_____

_____

_____

_____

_____

_____

_____

_____

_____

_____

In small groups, you might want to discuss some of the ideas that you have written in your journal.

Endnotes

Chapter 1

1. McCrum, Robert, William Cran, and Robert MacNeil. *The Story of English*. Viking Publishers, 1986, p. 20.

2. McCrum, p. 20.

3. Bryson, Bill. *The Mother Tongue: English & How It Got That Way*, p. 181.

4. Bryson, p. 182.

5. Bryson, p. 181

6. McCrum, p. 20

7. McCrum, p. 20

8. McCrum, p. 20

Chapter 2

1. Dolphin, Ric. "Breaking Away," *Maclean's*, March 13, 1989, p. 46.

2. Dolphin, p. 46.

3. Dolphin, p. 46

4. Cooper, Matthew, et al. "Empire of the Sun," *U.S. News and World Report*, May 28, 1990, pp. 44–51.

5. Cooper, et al. p. 44.

6. Fennell, Tom, et al. "A Financial Wave," *Maclean's*, November 18, 1991, p. 58.

7. Fennell, et al. p. 62.

8. McGlinn, Evan, "Good News for the Balance of Payments," *Forbes*, June 25, 1990, p. 37.

9. Dolphin, p. 46.

Chapter 3

1. Margolis, Mac. "Slowing Down the Destruction," *Maclean's*, December 16, 1991, p. 34.
2. Killian, Linda. "Jungle Fervor," *Forbes*, July 22, 1991, p. 315.
3. Baker, Lawrence, et al. "Acidic Lakes and Streams in the United States: The Role of Acidic Deposition," *Science* 252 (1991), pp. 1151–1152.
4. Monastersky, Richard. "Arctic Ozone Succumbs to Chemical Assault," *Science News*, March 24, 1990, p. 183.
5. Roan, Sharon. "Patching the Hole in the Sky: How to Eliminate Ozone-Damaging Chemicals from your Home," *Better Homes and Gardens*, June 1990, p. 106.
6. Monastersky, Richard. "Nations to Ban Ozone-Harming Compounds," *Science News*, July 7, 1990, p. 6.

Chapter 5

1. Guralnik, David B., ed. *Webster's New World Dictionary*, 2d ed., Simon & Schuster, 1982, p. 258.

Chapter 6

1. "Baha'i," *Academic American Encyclopedia*, 1988 ed.
2. Brown, W. Norman. "Hinduism," *The Encyclopedia Americana International Edition*, 1985 ed.
3. Vucinich, Wayne S. "Islam," *Collier's Encyclopedia*, 1993 ed.
4. Roth, Cecil. "Judaism," *Merit Students Encyclopedia*, 1990 ed.
5. Kitagawa, Joseph M., and John S. Strong. "Buddhism," *Academic American Encyclopedia*, 1988 ed.

Chapter 7

1. Cleveland, Harlan. "Rethinking International Governance: Coalition Politics in an Unruly World," *The Futurist*, May–June 1991, pp. 22–23.

2. Witman, Shepherd L. "League of Nations," *Collier's Encyclopedia*, 1993 ed.

3. Stoessinger, John G. "United Nations," *Academic American Encyclopedia*, 1988 ed.

Chapter 8

1. Reisman, W. Michael. "International Law," *Academic American Encyclopedia*, 1988 ed.

2. Osmanczyk, Edmund Jan. "International Law," *Encyclopedia of the United Nations and International Agreements*, 1990 ed. p. 457.

3. Reisman, W. Michael. "International Law," *Academic American Encyclopedia*, 1988 ed., pp. 11, 221.

4. Bledsoe, Robert L., and Boleslaw A. Boczek. *The International Law Dictionary*, ABC-CLIO Publishers, 1987, p. 222.

5. Bledsoe and Boczek, p. 176.

6. Osmanczyk, Edmund Jan. "International Court of Justice ICJ," *Encyclopedia of the United Nations and International Agreements*, 1990 ed., pp. 447–448.

Chapter 9

1. Fraser, Stewart E. "International Education," *Encyclopedia Americana International Edition*, 1985 ed.

2. Smolowe, Jill. "The Pursuit of Excellence," *Time*, April 13, 1992, pp. 59–60.

3. Quinn, Hal. "Canada by Choice," *Maclean's*, November 11, 1991, pp. 83–85.

4. Leslie, Connie, Carol Hall, and Ruth Marshall, "Global Market, by Degrees," *Newsweek*, March 8, 1993, p. 65.

Chapter 10

1. C.P. "The Taste of Things to Come," *Prevention*, January 1990, pp. 38–40, 117, 120–121.

2. Uher, Richard A. "Levitating Trains," *The Futurist*, September/ October 1990, pp. 28–32.

3. Perlmutter, Cathy. "You, the New Activated Patient," *Prevention*, January 1990, pp. 34–36.

Bibliography

"Baha'i." *Academic American Encyclopedia,* 1988 ed.

Baker, Lawrence A., et al. "Acidic Lakes and Streams in the United States: The Role of Acidic Deposition." *Science,* 252 (1991), 1151–1154.

Bledsoe, Robert L., and Boleslaw A. Boczek. *The International Law Dictionary.* Santa Barbara, Calif.: ABC-CLIO Publishers, 1987.

Blumthaler, Mario. and Walter Ambach. "Indication of Increasing Solar Ultraviolet-B Radiation Flux in Alpine Regions." *Science,* 248 (1990), 206–208.

Bower, Bruce. "Culture puts Unique Spin on Moral Judgment." *Science News,* May 2, 1992, p. 295.

Brown, W. Norman. "Hinduism." *The Encyclopedia Americana International Edition.* 1985 ed.

Bryson, Bill. *The Mother Tongue: English & How It Got That Way.* New York: William Morrow and Company, Inc., 1990.

Cetron, Marvin, and Owen Davies. "50 Trends Shaping the World." *The Futurist.* September/October 1991, pp. 11–21.

"Christianity." *The New Encyclopaedia Britannica,* 1986 ed.

Cleveland, Harlan. "Rethinking International Governance: Coalition Politics in an Unruly World." *The Futurist,* May–June 1991, pp. 20–27.

Cooper, Matthew, Dorian Friedman, and John Loenig. "Empire of the Sun." *U.S. News and World Report,* May 28, 1990, pp. 44–51.

Dolphin, Ric. Breaking Away." *Maclean's,* March 13, 1989, pp. 46–47.

Fennell, Tom, et al. "A Financial Wave." *Maclean's,* November 18, 1991, pp. 58–62.

Fraser, Stewart E. "International Education." *Encyclopedia Americana International Edition,*. 1985 ed.

Grinling, Kenneth. "World Health Organization." *Encyclopedia Americana International Edition,* 1985 ed.

Guralnik, David B. ed. *Webster's New World Dictionary.* 1982 ed.

Howard, Beth. "The Great Terrain Robbery: An Outdated Law is Wreaking Havoc on the Western Wilderness." *Omni Magazine,* June 1991, p. 20.

Kidder, Rushworth M. "Ethics: A Matter of Survivial." *The Futurist*, March/April 1992, pp. 10–12.

Killian, Linda. "Jungle Fervor." *Forbes*, July 22, 1991, p. 315.

Kitagawa, Joseph M., and John S. Strong. "Buddhism." *Academic American Encyclopedia,* 1988 ed.

Kuehnelt-Leddihn, Erik Von. "Xenophobia on the March." *National Review*, January 22, 1990, p. 44.

Leslie, Connie, Carol Hall, and Ruth Marshall. "Global Market, by Degrees." *Newsweek*, March 8, 1993, p. 65.

Margolis, Mac. "Slowing Down the Destruction." *Maclean's*, December 16, 1991, p. 34.

McCrum, Robert, William Cran, and Robert MacNeil. *The Story of English*. New York: Viking Publishers, 1986.

McGlinn, Evan. "Good News for the Balance of Payments." *Forbes*, June 25, 1990, pp. 36–38.

Monastersky, Richard. "Antarctic Ozone Bottoms at Record Low." *Science News*, October 13, 1990 p. 228.

Monastersky, Richard. "Arctic Ozone Succumbs to Chemical Assault." *Science News*, March 24, 1990, p. 183.

Monastersky, Richard. "Nations to Ban Ozone-harming Compounds." *Science News*, July 7, 1990, p. 6.

Monastersky, Richard. "The Warped World of Mental Maps." *Science News*, October 3, 1992, pp. 222–223.

Osmanczyk, Edmund Jan. "International Court of Justice ICJ." *Encyclopedia of the United Nations and International Agreements*. 1990 ed.

Osmanczyk, Edmund Jan. "International Law." *Encyclopedia of the United Nations and International Agreements*. 1990 ed.

Perlmutter, Cathy. "You, the New Activated Patient." *Prevention*, January 1990, pp. 34–36.

Plano, Jack C., and Roy Olton. *The International Relations Dictionary*. New York: Holt, Rinehart and Winston, Inc., 1969.

Quinn, Hal. "Canada by Choice." *Maclean's*, November 11, 1991, pp. 83–85.

Reisman, W. Michael. "International Law." *Academic American Encyclopedia,* 1988 ed.

Roan, Sharon. "Patching the Hole in the Sky: How to Eliminate Ozone-damaging Chemicals from your Home." *Better Homes and Gardens,* June 1990, p. 106.

Rossman, Parker. "The Emerging Global University." *The Futurist,* November/December 1991, pp. 19–20.

Roth, Cecil. "Judaism." *Merit Students Encyclopedia,* 1990 ed.

Smolowe, Jill, et al. "The Pursuit of Excellence." *Time,* April 13, 1992, pp. 59–60.

Stoessinger, John G. "United Nations." *Academic American Encyclopedia,* 1988 ed.

Stoessinger, John G. "World Health Organization." *Academic American Encyclopedia,* 1988 ed.

"The Taste of Things to Come." *Prevention,* January 1990, pp. 38–40, 117, 120–121.

Uher, Richard A. "Levitating Trains." *The Futurist,* September–October 1990, pp. 28–32.

Vucinich, Wayne S. "Islam." *Collier's Encyclopedia,* 1993 ed.

Waldrop, Judith. "You'll Know it's the 21st Century When ..." *The Saturday Evening Post,* April 1991, pp. 68–71, 111.

Weisman, Steven R. "Doing the Needful." *New York Times Magazine,* July 12, 1987, pp. 6–8.

Witman, Shepherd L. "League of Nations." *Collier's Encyclopedia,* 1993 ed.